# IT'S TIME TO MOVE FROM

# *Ponder*

## TO

# *Purpose*

*A Biblical Guide to Connect with God's Purposes from the Book of Nehemiah*

## DENA CRECY

# Contents

# Introduction

"For I know the plans I have for you," declares the Lord, "plans to prosper you and not to harm you, plans to give you hope and a future."
*Jeremiah 29:11 (NIV)*

Whether you are in church or not, you have probably heard this verse recited before. If you are a Christian or Christ follower, prayerfully you believe this is true. However, even for those of us who believe it is true, we sometimes find it hard to believe that it is true for *us*, in particular.

We see people on social media platforms doing all of these amazing things and ponder the questions, *Why not me? Where is my, "big thing" that I should be doing? Did God forget about me?* I can assure you that based on His word, He has not.

In his book, *In Pursuit of Purpose*, Dr. Myles Munroe states there is a purpose for everything God has created.[1] This goes along with Jeremiah 29:11. Dr. Munroe also states that every purpose is not known. He refers to the hair under our arms that we shave off. He also mentions several kinds of bugs and insects, like cockroaches. We don't know the purpose of cockroaches, but since they are one of God's creations, they must have a purpose.

For humans, it is not always so cut and dry as it is with things God created that are not human. We have twists and turns as we connect and spend time with God for Him to reveal our purpose(s) to us. The Bible has several examples of people's journeys to purpose. There's Adam and Eve, Moses, Abraham, and Joseph, to name a few.

God's purpose for you will be something you are passionate about, and you will do it whether you get paid to do it or not. Most people try to make their passion their vocation. I know I did when I first gave my life to Christ. I made up my mind that I was going to work at my

---

[1] Munroe, Myles. *In Pursuit of Purpose: The Key to Personal Fulfillment.* Destiny Image, 1992.

church in Houston or go into full-time ministry. That thinking almost got me fired. I was a very young Christian.

I was working at a bank. This was my first job after my separation from my husband and before the divorce. It started as a part-time position, which was fine with me because, again, I was only passing through there on my way to full-time ministry. It was a customer service job, and I did just enough to get by. When I would have my one-on-ones with my manager and she asked me what my goals were for the company, my response would be that I had no goals for this company and I'm only passing through on my way to full-time ministry. She would share how she saw leadership capabilities in me, and she knew I could perform at a higher level that I was currently performing. I worked from 10:00 a.m. to 2:00 p.m. and was late every day. I did not represent the Kingdom of God at all. Again, baby Christian.

As time went on, I found myself on a final, final, final write up for my tardiness. After 15 months had gone by, my manager said I should reevaluate my goal because it looks like God has something here for me to do. I was convicted right then and there. I confessed and repented to God and received His forgiveness. I began to "do my work heartily as unto the Lord, rather than for man," as stated in Colossians 3:3–24. I moved to a full-time position and was with that company for 15 years! I laugh out loud when I think about that time in my life and how God protected me from myself. I know my manager must have thought I was crazy! Thank God for using her to get me straight!

I shared that story because I've learned that for me and my journey to purpose, my job was simply a tool to provide for my family. I was still afforded the opportunity to pursue purpose and live out my passion, once discovered. There are several examples of this in the Bible, where a vocation was just a vocation, a job for payment, and God's calling was something different.

In this writing, we will look at the first six chapters of Nehemiah to see his journey to purpose and what we can glean from it. I share the chapters in this particular book as they are relatable to me.

While you are reading, ask yourself, *What burdens me? What am I passionate about?* If nothing comes to mind, then it's time to reconnect with God through His Word because He *does* have a plan for you.

# CHAPTER ONE

# Prayer, Passion & Purpose

## Nehemiah's Prayer

### CHAPTER ONE

¹ The words of Nehemiah son of Hakaliah:

In the month of Kislev in the twentieth year, while I was in the citadel of Susa, ² Hanani, one of my brothers, came from Judah with some other men, and I questioned them about the Jewish remnant that had survived the exile, and also about Jerusalem.

[3] They said to me, "Those who survived the exile and are back in the province are in great trouble and disgrace. The wall of Jerusalem is broken down, and its gates have been burned with fire."

[4] When I heard these things, I sat down and wept. For some days I mourned and fasted and prayed before the God of heaven. [5] Then I said:

"LORD, the God of heaven, the great and awesome God, who keeps his covenant of love with those who love him and keep his commandments, [6] let your ear be attentive and your eyes open to hear the prayer your servant is praying before you day and night for your servants, the people of Israel. I confess the sins we Israelites, including myself and my father's family, have committed against you. [7] We have acted very wickedly toward you. We have not obeyed the commands, decrees and laws you gave your servant Moses.

[8] "Remember the instruction you gave your servant Moses, saying, 'If you are unfaithful, I will scatter you among the nations, [9] but if you return to me and obey my commands, then even if your exiled people are at the farthest horizon, I will gather

them from there and bring them to the place I have chosen as a dwelling for my Name.'

[10] "They are your servants and your people, whom you redeemed by your great strength and your mighty hand. [11] Lord, let your ear be attentive to the prayer of this your servant and to the prayer of your servants who delight in revering your name. Give your servant success today by granting him favor in the presence of this man."

I was cupbearer to the king. (NIV)

After Nehemiah heard the news about what was going on back home, it bothered him so much that he sat down and wept and mourned for many days. It bothered him so much that he began to pray for favor. It bothered him so much that he prayed for God to allow him to do something about it. He prayed for success and favor with "this man"—his boss, the king.

His prayer included confession of sins, not just for the Israelites, but for himself and his family as well as his father's family. After he wept and mourned the situation, he poured out his heart to God. He felt bad for his people not having covering and being exposed. He did not move on his own or lean on his own understanding. He waited for God's *yes*, *no*, or *not now*.

## Questions to Ponder:

What do you hear about or see that makes you weep and mourn?

What kinds of things burden you or send you to the Lord in prayer?

For me, it is people in non-peaceful relationships. People who were once in love are now at war with each other. When I hear about abuse in relationships or hear about separation or divorce, it makes me sad.

Or, watching single women (and men) doing things outside of what they say they believe in order to have a relationship—any kind of relationship. I noticed it when I was 15 years old, working my first job as a certified nurse's assistant. A young adult coworker approached me about taking in her and her 6-month-old daughter because she was being abused by her husband. She was from Arizona and knew no one in Houston except him. I had to ask my mom, and she said yes. For four years, I watched physical, verbal, and emotional abuse take place between them. My coworker (now lifelong friend of over 50 years) was in nursing school to be a registered nurse and wanted to finish before going back home to Arizona. She completed nursing school and became a registered nurse. They got a divorce and, thankfully, that was the end of the relationship.

This was during my pre-Christ days. Once I gave my life to Christ at 24, I noticed that I discerned abuse more. I noticed it was subtle (*more verbal and emotional than physical*) and all around me. Yes, even in the faith community.

The sadness grew deeper, and I began to earnestly pray and ask God what, if anything, I could do about it. By this time, I had been married for four years. Shortly thereafter, my own marriage was added to my prayer list and needed intervention from God.

## Nehemiah's Passion

"When I heard these things, I sat down and wept. For some days I mourned and fasted and prayed before the God of Heaven."
Nehemiah 1:4 (NIV)

**Webster's definition of passion:** a strong feeling of enthusiasm or excitement for or devotion to some activity, object, or concept

**Spiritual definition of passion:** "Passion" has to do with our heart—the internal fire that motivates us and energizes us to fulfil our purpose and do God's will. God is the source of spiritual passion. The Holy Spirit comes to ignite us with holy fire. In the world we live in, natural passion is often a key to success and impact.

Likewise, the scriptures urge us to live our lives with passion. The Apostle Paul encourages believers to "never be lacking in zeal" (Romans 12:11). Later on, in his letter to the Galatians, he says to them, "It is good to be zealous, provided the purpose is good" (Galatians 4:18).

God will give you a passion or burden for something bigger than you. He will light a fire in you for the particular task that's bothering you. He will use you to solve a particular problem. This passion or burden that is from God will not leave you alone. It may lie dormant for some time, but it will not completely go away. It will keep coming back up. It will move you to action.

We as believers in Jesus Christ are called to something to advance His Kingdom, something that will bring Him glory. Jesus said in John 17:4, "I glorified You on earth, having accomplished the work which You have given me to do." We can read in Acts 13:36, "For David, after he had served the purposes of God in his own generation, fell asleep, and was laid among is fathers and underwent decay." I want—and I pray you want as well—for it to be said that we served the purposes of God in our generation.

It doesn't matter how raggedy our lives are; we can still be used by God to carry out His specific purpose(s) for our lives. All of Jesus' disciples—the ones He handpicked—left Him during the crucifixion, but they all (except Judas) came back and were used to spread the gospel and bring people to Christ. We cannot believe the enemy's lie that we cannot be used by God, that we have messed up too badly to be used by Him. We have not.

As we read the Bible, most of the people God used had some kind of issue. Luke 22:31–32 says, "Simon, Simon, Satan has asked to sift all of you as wheat. But I have prayed for you, Simon, that your faith may not fail. And when you have turned back, strengthen your brothers." We could put our name where Simon's name is. Satan is God's satan. He has to ask for permission to "sift us as wheat." Thankfully, Jesus said, "But I have prayed for you, that your faith may not fail." Jesus prayed that *our faith* may not fail, not that *we* wouldn't fail, because we will. The goal of the enemy is to separate us from our faith. Faith is holding on to what God has already said. But first, we must know what He has said by reading His word. Psalm 119:11 says, "I have hidden your word in my heart that I might not sin against you." This verse says that I *might not* sin against You; it doesn't say we won't sin.

Luke 22:32 goes on to say that when you have turned back, strengthen your brothers. *When* you turn back, not *if* you turn back. And Simon Peter did just that, bringing about three thousand souls to Christ on the day of Pentecost as it states in Acts 2:41.

It's time to receive the passion God has put inside of you and allow Him to ignite it to serve the purposes of God in your generation.

## Nehemiah's Purpose/Assignment

### CHAPTER 2:2–5

[2] so the king asked me, "Why does your face look so sad when you are not ill? This can be nothing but sadness of heart."

I was very much afraid, [3] but I said to the king, "May the king live forever! Why should my face not look sad when the city where my ancestors are buried lies in ruins, and its gates have been destroyed by fire?"

[4] The king said to me, "What is it you want?"

Then I prayed to the God of heaven, [5] and I answered the king, "If it pleases the king and if your servant has found favor in his sight, let him send me to the city in Judah where my ancestors are buried so that I can rebuild it." (NIV)

In this chapter, Nehemiah's assignment, he believed, was to go home and rebuild the walls and the gates that had been burned with fire. He continued to pray about it as he conversed with the King. He was seeking God for confirmation and favor and the king (his boss) for permission.

As the book of Nehemiah progresses, he had other assignments in addition to the rebuilding of the walls and gates. Some of us have multiple assignments while on this earth, and some may just have one huge assignment, but God is in control of them all.

As previously referenced In Acts 13:36, the Bible says, "Now when David had served God's purpose in his own generation, he fell asleep; he was buried with his ancestors and his body decayed." David did have many assignments in his lifetime, and they were not called out separately at the end of his life. It says when he had served God's purpose in his own generation, he fell asleep.

When God gives you an assignment, He will confirm it by giving you favor as you move forward.

# CHAPTER TWO

# Opportunity & Purpose

## CHAPTER 2:6

<sup></sup> Then the king, with the queen sitting beside him, asked me, "How long will your journey take, and when will you get back?" It pleased the king to send me; so, I set a time. (NIV)

Nehemiah's boss, King Artaxerxes, gave him time off to go back home and rebuild the walls. This is the same King that stopped the walls from being rebuilt back in Ezra chapter 4 in response to accusations from Samarian officials that the city was rebellious. This is evidence that a no, or blockage, can be reversed by God when the people come together and fast and pray. When God wants us to do something, He will make it clear and confirm by creating an opportunity to do it. We don't have to force it or make it happen.

When I left my corporate job in 2015, I believed God wanted me to set up the nonprofit I believe He had given me, *Relationships God Style*. I had taken a few classes in previous years on how to set one up. One of those classes was how to apply for nonprofit status at the state level, which is required in Texas before applying with the IRS. I applied for and was approved at the state level in December 2010. I applied for and was approved with the IRS in June of 2015. I was excited and started looking for office space to see clients. There was a space in the city of Cedar Hill that I was able to secure in August of 2015. (More on the office space when we get to provision in the next chapter.)

I went to Seminary and graduated with a master's degree in theological studies and was licensed and ordained as a minister. My goal was to be able to not only do premarital coaching but also officiate weddings. My first wedding was in 2010 with my previous Director that I supported before leaving the company. Once he heard I was a licensed minister, he asked if I would do their premarital coaching and officiate their wedding in December of 2010. That was confirmation for me that I was going down the right path.

Since then, God has provided many opportunities for me to do premarital coaching sessions and officiate weddings. Most of them were for the people I previously worked with, the marketplace.

At every turn, I had opportunities confirmed by God. In 2016, I became a member of a local author's group and was named or appointed the Chaplain of the group. I didn't really know what a Chaplain was. I researched it and accepted the appointment. In 2021, my pastor mentioned that the ministers of the church should look into becoming a Chaplain. So, I began researching Chaplain training schools and found *Christians in the Marketplace*. That name, as well as the price, was confirmation for me. I believe God has called me to marketplace ministry. I enrolled in the Fall of 2022 and graduated with the highest score in the class of 95%. This was confirmation that I was where God wanted me to be.

Proverbs 18:16 says, "A man's gift makes room for him, and brings him before great men" (NASB).

This means your unique talents, skills, and abilities create opportunities, open doors, and bring you recognition and influence with important people, essentially making a path for success and purpose. It suggests that by developing and using what you're good at, you'll find fulfillment, gain access to powerful circles, and fulfill your potential, as illustrated by biblical figures like Joseph, who used his gift to interpret dreams to gain favor with the Pharaoh.

## Key meanings and applications:

*Opportunity Creation:*

Your abilities naturally attract attention and opportunities that wouldn't exist otherwise, acting as a key to unlocking new spaces. I love to serve as it brings me great joy. This was the case even before my pre-Christ days.

Everywhere I have served, I have been offered various opportunities to serve outside of the position where I started. While serving in the kitchen at a local family shelter, the Director of the Women's program asked me if I would be a mentor. It was in line with my gifts, skills, and abilities, so I agreed. She then asked if would facilitate a workforce development class, focusing on resume creation and review, along with interview preparation.

This was definitely in my wheelhouse, so I agreed. While facilitating the weekly classes, the CEO asked if I could lead chapel on Friday mornings. Another opportunity that aligned with my gifts, skills, and abilities, so I agreed. My manager was very supportive of me and allowed me to participate.

These experiences reinforce Proverbs 18:16 to me. There is something that Jesus says in Matthew 9:37–38: "The harvest is plentiful, but the workers are few. Therefore, plead with the Lord of the harvest to send out workers into His harvest" (NASB).

## Access to Influence:

The verse alludes to ancient customs where gifts gained an audience with rulers; similarly, your talents can bring you before "great men" or leaders in your field.

## Purpose Fulfillment:

Activating your gift isn't just about success; it's about fulfilling a divine purpose.

## Divine Provision:

It's a principle of divine providence, suggesting God equips individuals with talents to bring them to their intended place and purpose.

## How to make room for your gifts:

- **Discover and Develop**: Identify your unique talents and actively work to improve them.

- **Activate and Steward**: Don't let your gifts lie dormant; use them faithfully to serve others and God.

- **Be Open to Growth**: Be willing to take small steps and grow your capacity to handle bigger opportunities

As you discover, develop, and use the unique talents and gifts God has given you for the advancement of His Kingdom, make sure you praise and thank Him for what He is doing in your life.

# CHAPTER THREE

# Provision & Purpose

## CHAPTER 2:7-9

⁷ I also said to him, "If it pleases the king, may I have letters to the governors of Trans-Euphrates, so that they will provide me safe-conduct until I arrive in Judah? ⁸ And may I have a letter to Asaph, keeper of the royal park, so he will give me timber to make beams for the gates of the citadel by the temple and for the city wall and for the residence I will occupy?" And because the gracious hand of my God was on me, the king granted my requests. ⁹ So I went to the governors of Trans-Euphrates and

gave them the king's letters. The king had also sent
army officers and cavalry with me. (NIV)

WOW! Nehemiah received all that he asked for and
more. God did exceedingly, abundantly more than he
asked for. He got a passport and timber to make beams
for the gates, city wall, and the residence he would occupy. He also had protection from the army. All that he
needed, God's hand provided. Nehemiah's prayer of favor was answered.

Nehemiah was not doing this for notoriety or fame.
He was doing this because it bothered him that his people back home were disgraced because the walls were
down. He rebuilt the walls of Jerusalem primarily for
physical security, national identity, and spiritual restoration, as the broken walls left the city vulnerable to enemies, brought shame to God, and symbolized the people's brokenness after exile. It was not about him, but
about doing what he believed God purposed him to do
for his people.

Now, back to the office space I mentioned in the previous chapter. This same person that I married in 2010
reached out to me in 2015 to find out what my plans were
moving forward and asked to meet for lunch. We met

and I shared my verbal plan as I believe God gave it to me. He said he believed in me and wanted to support me. He asked how much the office space was and what other first-year expenses I had. He then wrote a check for the first month expenses discussed. That was another confirmation that I was headed in the right direction. I was and still am praising God as I didn't know how I was going to fund that office space. It was a step of faith. God confirmed that decision, and I am still praising Him for it!

God provides for what He wants done. He provided for Adam and Eve in the garden. He provided a ram in the bush to Abraham so he would not kill his son. Noah received instructions and provisions when he was asked to build an Ark. He provided for Moses and the Israelites as He led them out of Egypt. God is a God of purpose, and His purposes will be carried out. He will use us to carry out His purposes, but they are never about us. They are about the people we are serving and the expansion of His Kingdom.

## Should I quit my job to go after God's purpose for me?

I have heard many people say that God told them to quit their job and start a ministry, and then struggle to live afterwards. I am not one to say that God did not say quit your job, but we must make sure we are on His timing. He told Joseph he would be in a position where people would bow down to him, even his family, but it took 13 years for that to happen. God will give us a glimpse and then prepare us to receive it.

When I believed God told me to leave my job in 2015, I took the severance package because God confirmed that I would not relocate with the company. I set up the nonprofit and took another job six months later. My traditional days of working were not done yet, as I had to take care of my obligations while I grew the nonprofit. The VP I used to work with paid for the office space and ministry expenses for the first year, but not my personal living expenses. Based on the examples in the Bible and my personal experience, I believe God funds what He fuels. Below are just a few examples from the Bible of God providing for purpose:

- **Elijah at the Brook Cherith in 1 Kings Chapter 17**

- **Moses speaking for the people in Exodus Chapter 3**

- Joshua taking over after Moses in Joshua Chapter 1

- Jeremiah preaching His word in Jeremiah Chapter 20

- **Noah building an Ark in Genesis Chapter 6**

There are so many other examples in the Bible to read about and learn from. All that were called faced protest and opposition but pressed through to God's desired outcome. It was not easy, but with God's help, they prevailed. The Bible is our encouragement to stick close to God and follow His lead. We must be careful of the spirit of comparison as it can get us distracted, lead us astray, and cause our faith in God to fail.

I will end this chapter with a quote I heard from a Pastor I listen to out of Maryland. He says, "Don't jump off the horse you are on unless another horse is coming by." In other words, don't quit one job or source of income until you have another one in place to sustain you. It doesn't mean you don't have faith; it just means you are being wise in your decisions.

# CHAPTER FOUR

# Protest & Purpose

## The Mockery & Scoffing (Nehemiah 2:19; 4:1-3)

*Showing political opposition:*

**Nehemiah 2:19**: "But when Sanballat the Horonite and Tobiah the Ammonite official, and Geshem the Arab heard it, they mocked us and despised us and said, 'What is this thing that you are doing? Are you rebelling against the king?'" (NASB)

*Scorned their ability:*

**Nehemiah 4:1–3**: "Sanballat was furious and ridiculed the Jews, saying, 'What are these feeble Jews doing? Will they restore it? Will they sacrifice? Will they finish in a day? Will they revive the stones from the heaps of rubbish—stones that are burned?'" (NASB)

## Plots & Threats (Nehemiah 4:7–11; 6:1–9)

*Direct military threat:*

**Nehemiah 4:7–8**: When Sanballat, Tobiah, the Arabs, Ammonites, and Ashdodites heard repairs were progressing, they "plotted together to come and fight against Jerusalem and to cause trouble for it" (NASB).

**Nehemiah 4:10–12**: Internal discouragement arose as people felt overwhelmed, and enemies spread rumors that attackers would come from all directions to kill them.

**Nehemiah 6:1–7**: Sanballat and others repeatedly tried to lure Nehemiah out of Jerusalem for a meeting, intending to harm him, and sent letters accusing him of plotting rebellion.

When you are doing the Lord's work, there will be mockery, scoffing, plots, and threats. Most, if not all, of the people in the Bible who carried out a work for the Lord met some kind of opposition.

## Old Testament Examples

- **Moses:** Initially hesitant, then powerfully resisted by Pharaoh, who refused to let the Israelites go despite the plagues.

- **Elijah:** Boldly challenged the prophets of Baal on Mount Carmel against King Ahab and Queen Jezebel's promotion of idolatry.

- **Jeremiah:** Persecuted, imprisoned, and thrown into a muddy cistern for prophesying against Jerusalem's sins.

## New Testament Examples

- **John the Baptist:** Confronted by the Pharisees and eventually beheaded by King Herod for denouncing his adultery.

- **Stephen:** The first Christian martyr, stoned to death by religious opponents, including a zealous

Saul (later Paul).

- **Jesus:** Faced constant opposition from religious leaders (Pharisees, Sadducees) and political powers, culminating in His crucifixion.

- **Paul:** Faced immense opposition, persecution, and attempts to discredit him from both Jewish and Gentile communities as he spread the Gospel.

These figures demonstrate that opposition is common in God's service, often coming from those who resist change, truth, or God's established order, requiring faith, prayer, and perseverance.

I can recall that every time God was transitioning me from one phase of life to another, something would happen. Each time I was up for promotion, I would be attacked. Once, my place was broken into and all that was taken was a hammer. Very strange. When I got ready to move from apartment life to my new home, the apartment was plagued with large flies on the windows every night I came home from work the week I was scheduled to move. It was very bizarre. I had never seen anything like it. There was much prayer, laying at His feet and reciting His word, as there were times I was scared to come home. I knew it was attack of the enemy.

My last published book (an anthology) was in 2024. It was nominated for an award through the Christian Literary Awards scheduled for April 2025. The week before the ceremony, the root from the tree in my front yard busted the main pipe and flooded my home. When that happened, I knew the book was going to win an award. Not a good experience. Then my daughter, who has never participated in any of my book events, called two days before the event to say that she and my granddaughter would attend the event. A good experience. The book won not just one award, but two! The Readers' Choice Award and the Henri Award! We were all so excited! The authors and I got together every Sunday evening and prayed for favor. God did exceedingly, abundantly beyond we could ask or think. It was a grand night.

Just know that the enemy is not going to let you, me, or us step into God's purpose without mockery, scoffing, plots, and threats.

## Nehemiah's Response & Prayer (Nehemiah 4:9–14; 6:16)

*Prayer and preparedness:*

**Nehemiah 4:9:** "We prayed to our God and posted a guard day and night to meet this threat." (NIV)

*Faith and defense:*

**Nehemiah 4:13–14:** He stationed guards with weapons (swords, spears, bows) behind the wall and encouraged the people: "Do not be afraid of them. Remember the Lord, who is great and glorious, and fight for your brothers, your sons, your daughters, your wives, and your homes!" (NIV)

**Nehemiah 6:15:** Together, they rebuilt the walls of Jerusalem in 52 days. Yes, the Bible states that Nehemiah and the people of Jerusalem rebuilt the city walls in a remarkable 52 days—a feat attributed to divine help, strong leadership, division of labor, and perseverance against opposition, even though the construction was hasty, as confirmed by archaeology.

**Nehemiah 6:16:** When enemies heard God had frustrated their plots, they were "frightened and humiliated," realizing the work was done with God's help. They knew he could not do it alone.

**Jesus said** in John 16:33, "I have told you these things, so that in me you may have peace. In this world you will have trouble. But take heart! I have overcome the world" (NIV).

# CHAPTER FIVE

# People & Purpose

## Nehemiah Chapter 2:17-18 & Nehemiah Chapter 3

*Context:*

**Before these verses (Nehemiah 2:16):** Nehemiah had secretly inspected Jerusalem's broken walls and gates after his arrival but hadn't revealed his plans to the Jewish leaders or workers.

**The Problem:** Jerusalem lay in ruins, its gates burned, making the people a "reproach" or object of ridicule.

*The Message in Nehemiah 2:17–18*

- **The Call (Verse 17):** Nehemiah points out their dire situation and proposes action: "Come, let us build the wall of Jerusalem, that we may no longer suffer derision/be a reproach!"

- **The Motivation (Verse 18):** He shares the divine backing for the project, explaining God's favor upon him and the king's supportive words.

- **The Response (Verse 18):** The people are inspired and declare, "Let us rise up and build!" They then "strengthened their hands for this good work," meaning they prepared and began with determination.

In essence, these verses mark the turning point where a shared vision, rooted in faith and practical need, ignites the community to action against overwhelming challenges.

**Nehemiah Chapter 3** details various groups and individuals—priests, Levites, rulers, common citizens, artisans (like goldsmiths and perfumers), and even women—working on different sections of the wall, from the Sheep Gate to the Water Gate, with specific sections assigned to each group. Key figures mentioned include Eliashib the high priest, Rehum, Hashabiah, Baruch, Meremoth, Azariah, and Benjamin and Hasshub, all working alongside their families and communities.

This is significant because God does not expect us to carry out His purpose or assignment alone. We need people to assist with various parts or phases of the project. We are not to be alone. We may be the project leader but should not attempt to execute it alone.

Noah had his family and probably some hired laborers as the task to build an ark was enormous. Moses had people. Joshua had people. Joseph had people. David had people. Jesus had people.

Calling out Moses, I'm reminded of a time in the Bible where Moses was handling all the issues the people had by himself. His father-in-law, Jethro, was observing and gave him some advice. Jethro advised him to delegate his judicial responsibilities to capable, trustworthy leaders, preventing Moses from burnout and improving efficiency for the Israelites, as described in Exodus 18:13–26. Jethro observed Moses judging all cases himself, recognized the task was too great, and suggested appointing leaders over thousands, hundreds, fifties, and tens to handle lesser disputes, bringing only difficult cases to Moses.

## Jethro's Key Advice (Exodus 18:17–23)

- **Identify the Problem:** "What you are doing is not good. You will surely wear out, both yourself and these people who are with you, for the task is too heavy for you; you cannot do it alone."

- **Provide a Solution:** "Now listen to me: I will give you counsel, and God be with you."

- **Delegate Authority:** Appoint capable men who fear God and are honest to be leaders over groups of 10, 50, 100, and 1,000.

- **Teach and Train:** Instruct these leaders in God's laws and decrees, showing them how to live and judge.

- **Handle Difficult Cases:** The appointed leaders should judge everyday matters, bringing only complex cases to Moses.

**Outcome:** Moses followed Jethro's counsel, appointing leaders, which relieved him of the overwhelming burden, allowed him more time with God, and created a more organized system for the people.

There are many other examples that show there are people to model after. We should collaborate and work in community. God will send the right people just for you and the task at hand.

I remember one time when I was moving from one apartment to another and I needed help. My children, who were school-aged at the time, and I had moved most of the furniture, but we could not move the washer and dryer. This is one of those times I felt alone after the divorce, being a single parent and feeling like I had to do everything by myself. I had asked a few people to help, but none of them were available.

I prayed about it and then had to make a Target run for something. There was this guy there that struck up a conversation with me. I was baffled because my appearance was not my usual self for going out in public. We conversed and I shared the need I had. He came over with a truck and a dolly and moved the washer and dryer for me, and I never saw him again. I know that was God answering my prayer for the current need I had. I normally don't engage with strangers like that, but I discerned this was God doing something, so I went with it. I thanked the guy and praised God when he left.

I was not surprised or disappointed that I never saw him again. All of the people that God allows to connect with us have different expiration dates. Some may stay a short time and some longer. God will move them on when it is time.

Some are there to pray for us and the task at hand. Some are there for encouragement. Some are there to converse with us, and some are there for other tasks regarding executing of the purpose. That was the case with Jesus and Judas. Jesus selected Judas knowing he was the one that was going to betray him. Technically, all of the disciples walked away from Jesus during the crucifixion, but they all came back (except Judas) and carried out their purpose of preaching the gospel.

And some are there to disrupt the purpose by mocking, scoffing, plotting, and offering up threats. As we stay close to God in prayer and abide in His word, He will reveal what we need to see and how we need to move.

In 1 Samuel 30:7, when all of the men spoke of stoning David when they came back to Ziklag and it had been burned and their family was gone, the Priest was the only one standing with him. The Priest provided the ministry of presence. He was there to hand him the ephod, a sacred vestment in ancient Israel, primarily worn by the High Priest, so he could make an inquiry of the Lord.

# The Men of Tekoa – Nehemiah 3:5, 27

**In Nehemiah 3**, the nobles of the Tekoites are specifically mentioned as the group who did not participate in the physical labor of rebuilding the wall, even though they lived nearby and would benefit from the increased security and restoration of the city.

**Nehemiah 3:5 states:** "Next to them the Tekoites made repairs, but their nobles would not put their shoulders to the work of their Lord" (NASB).

*Key details about these individuals:*

- **Pride and Arrogance:** Commentaries suggest the nobles likely considered manual labor beneath their social status and position, a sign of pride and unwillingness to "stoop to serve their Lord."

- **Contrast with the Common People:** Their refusal stands in sharp contrast to the rest of the people from Tekoa, who were diligent and even repaired a second section of the wall to compensate for their leaders' absence (Nehemiah 3:27).

- **Lack of Humility:** The phrase "put not their necks to the work" is a metaphor for a refusal to submit to the collective mission and leadership of Nehemiah's appointed supervisors.

The passage highlights that while the vast majority of people—including priests, merchants, goldsmiths, and various leaders—worked together with unity and commitment, the Tekoite nobles were a notable exception. Their inactivity is recorded in the biblical text as a negative example of failing to contribute to a community effort that served the common good and the work of God.

There will be some Tekoites that get with the crowd but will not "put their necks to the work." It will probably be for some of the reasons previously listed. Their pride and lack of humility will not allow them obey appointed leadership and do physical labor. God will show them to you as you stay connected to Him.

Everything I have accomplished in my life is because I have allowed God to send people to come alongside me and support me, even before I knew it was God during my life before Christ. My nonprofit is called "Relationships God Style." God gave me that name to confirm that I am not alone and my purpose is to come alongside to let others know they are not alone.

# CHAPTER SIX

# God & Purpose

Referring to Dr. Munroe's book again, *In Pursuit of Purpose*, he says, "Your fulfillment in life is dependent on your becoming and doing what you were born to be and do". He also says, "Find out who you are and be yourself."

1 Corinthians 9:26 states, "Therefore I do not run like someone running aimlessly; I do not fight like a boxer beating the air" (NIV).

In Proverbs 29:18, King Solomon states, "Where there is no vision, the people are unrestrained. But happy is one who keeps the Law" (NASB).

## What is Purpose?

According to Dr. Munroe, *purpose* is the original intent for the creation of a thing, the original reason for the existence of a thing, the end for which the means exist, the cause for the creation of a thing, the desired result that initiates production, the need that makes a manufacturer produce a specific product, the destination that prompts the journey, the expectation of the source, the objective for the subject, the aspiration for the inspiration, and the object one wills or resolves to have. All things begin and end with purpose, including mankind.

Dr. Munroe also states in his book that every purpose is not known to mankind. There is so much meat and scripture in his book *In Pursuit of Purpose* that I suggest you read it. It will be a good jump start or continuation of your pursuit of your God-ordained purpose. I will list the 7 Principles from his book to inspire you to read it:

*Principle #1*

God is a God of Purpose. God never made anything for the fun of it.

## Principle #2

Everything in life has a purpose. Ignorance of purpose does not cancel out purpose.

## Principle #3

Not every purpose is known. Not knowing the *why* doesn't mean that the thing, event, or person doesn't have a purpose; its purpose just isn't known.

## Principle #4

Wherever purpose is now known, abuse is inevitable. Abuse occurs whenever we don't use something according to its creator's intentions.

I want to interject here because we are living in a time where abuse is running rampant. There is domestic abuse or intimate partner violence. There is child abuse. There is senior abuse. There is sexual abuse. As Dr. Munroe states, abuse occurs whenever we don't use something according to its creator's intentions.

Abuse is all around us, and with social media, I see it increasing every day. That is the purpose of Relationships God Style: to share what the Bible says about how we should treat each other. I still believe the song written by Burt Bacharach and Hal David titled, "What the

World Needs Now Is Love". In addition to that, I believe the world needs individuals to discover and live out their purpose.

> "Where there is no vision, the people are unrestrained."
> Proverbs 29:18 (NASB)

> "When people do not accept divine guidance, they run wild."
> Proverbs 29:18 (NLT)

### What is God's intention for how we should treat each other?

The Bible teaches us to treat others with love, kindness, humility, and respect, summarized by the Golden Rule: "Do to others as you would have them do to you" (Matthew 7:12, Luke 6:31). This means forgiving enemies, praying for persecutors, serving one another, showing compassion, and valuing others above yourself, following Jesus' example of selfless love.

### Core Principles

- **The Golden Rule:** Treat people the way you want to be treated (Matthew 7:12, Luke 6:31).

- **Love and Forgiveness:** Love your enemies, bless those who curse you, and forgive others as God has forgiven you (Luke 6:27–28, Ephesians 4:32). The Bible says love, not like. You can love the human being, but not like the person or their behavior. It's not easy, but it is doable.

- **Humility and Service:** Be humble, don't be selfish, and consider others better than yourselves (Philippians 2:3–4).

- **Kindness and Compassion:** Be kind, tenderhearted, and build each other up (Ephesians 4:32, 1 Thessalonians 5:11).

- **Justice and Respect:** Treat strangers like natives and honor those deserving respect (Leviticus 19:33–34, Romans 13:7).

- **No Partiality:** Treat everyone the same, regardless of their status (James 2).

*Key Teachings in Practice*

- **Help the Needy:** Show compassion and care for others.

- **Speak Kindly:** Use words that heal, not wound (Proverbs 12:18).

- **Put Others First:** Serve one another through love (Galatians 5:13).

- **Examine Yourself:** Before judging others, deal with your own faults (Matthew 7:5).

## Principle #5

If you want to know the purpose of a thing, never ask the thing. A created thing can never know what was in the mind of the creator when he planned and built it.

## Principle #6

Purpose is only found in the mind of the creator. Only God knows the purpose for your life.

## Principle #7

Purpose is the key to fulfillment. Purpose dictates performance, which influences satisfaction. Thus, purpose is the key to fulfillment.

God has three general purposes for all who follow Him:

1. To know God. We get to know Him through His word (John 17:3).

2. To be conformed to His image (Romans 8:29).

3. To make Him known to others (Matthew 28:19–20).

In order to discover your purpose, abiding with God through His word is a start. In order to hear and receive from God, a relationship with His Son Jesus Christ is required. The next chapter provides an opportunity to invite Jesus in your life for the first time or rededicate your life back to Him. It is time to allow Him to be Savior and Lord. Time to move from ponder to purpose.

# A Message of Salvation to All

I am so glad that you purchased this project. As you are reading through the chapters, I don't want to assume that everyone reading this is a believer in God through Jesus Christ. This book is about the love of God in the Holy Bible, and I want you to experience this same love to the fullest by moving from pondering about purpose to receiving and executing it for the glory of God.

# THE FOUR SPIRITUAL LAWS

 God loves you.

 We are sinful and separated from God.

 Only through Jesus Christ can you know and experience God's love and salvation.

 We must receive Jesus Christ as Savior and Lord.

## 1. God loves you and created you to know Him personally.

### God's Love

> "For God so loved the world, that He gave His only Son, so that everyone who believes in Him will not perish, but have eternal life."
>
> *John 3:16*

### God's Plan

"And this is eternal life, that they may know You, the only true God, and Jesus Christ whom You have sent." (John 17:3). What prevents us from knowing God personally?

# 2. Man is sinful and separated from God, so we cannot know Him personally or experience His love.

### Man is Sinful

"All have sinned and fall short of the glory of God" (Romans 3:23). Man was created to have fellowship with God, but because of his own stubborn self-will, he chose to go his own independent way and fellowship with God was broken. This self-will, characterized by an attitude of active rebellion or passive indifference, is evidence of what the Bible calls sin.

### Man is Separated

"The wages of sin is death" [spiritual separation from God] (Romans 6:23). "Those who do not obey the gospel of our Lord Jesus... will pay the penalty of eternal destruction, away from the presence of the Lord and from the glory of His power" (2 Thessalonians 1:8–9).

The diagram on the next page illustrates that God is holy and man is sinful. A great gulf separates the two. The arrows illustrate that man is continually trying to reach God and establish the personal relationship with Him through his own efforts, such as a good life, philosophy, or religion—but he inevitably fails. The third principle explains the only way to bridge this gulf...

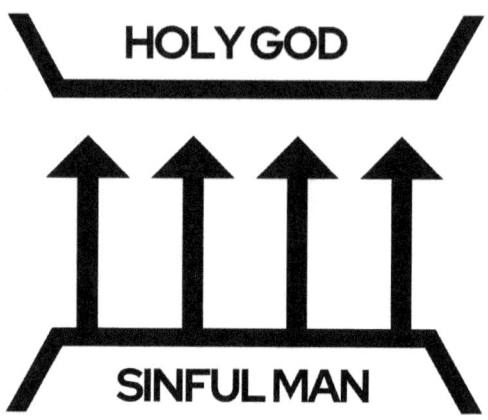

## 3. Jesus Christ is God's only provision for man's sin. Through Him alone we can know God personally and experience God's love.

### He Died in Our Place

> "But God demonstrates His own love toward us, in that while we were still sinners, Christ died for us:"
>
> *Romans 5:8*

### He Rose from the Dead

> "Christ died for our sins... He was buried... He was raised on the third day according to the Scriptures...

> He appeared to Cephas, then to the twelve. After that He appeared to more than five hundred..."
>
> *1 Corinthians 15:3–6*

**He is the Only Way to God**

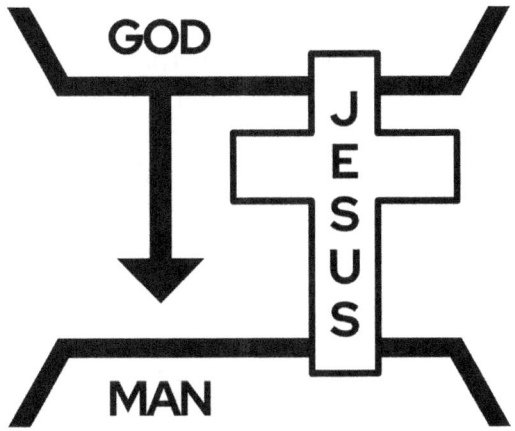

> "Jesus said to him, 'I am the way, and the truth, and the life; no one comes to the Father except through Me.'"
>
> *John 14:6*

This diagram illustrates that God has bridged the gulf that separates us from Him by sending His Son, Jesus Christ, to die on the cross in our place to pay the penalty for our sins.

**It is not enough just to know these truths...**

## 4. We must individually receive Jesus Christ as Savior and Lord; then we can know God personally and experience His love.

### We Must Receive Christ

> "But as many as received Him, to them He gave the right to become children of God, to those who believe in His name."
>
> *John 1:12*

### We Receive Christ Through Faith

> "For by grace you have been saved through faith; and this is not of yourselves, it is the gift of God; not a result of works, so that no one may boast."
>
> *Ephesians 2:8–9*

When we receive Christ, we experience a new birth (read John 3:1–8.)

### We Receive Christ by Personal Invitation

Jesus said, "Behold, I stand at the door and knock; if anyone hears My voice and opens the door, I will come

in to him and will dine with him, and he with Me"
(Revelation 3:20).

Receiving Christ involves turning to God from self
(repentance) and trusting Christ to come into our lives to
forgive us of our sins and to make us what He wants us
to be. Just to agree intellectually that Jesus Christ is the
Son of God and that He died on the cross for our sins is
not enough. Nor is it enough to have an emotional
experience. We receive Jesus Christ by faith, as an act of
our will.

## These two circles represent two kinds of lives:

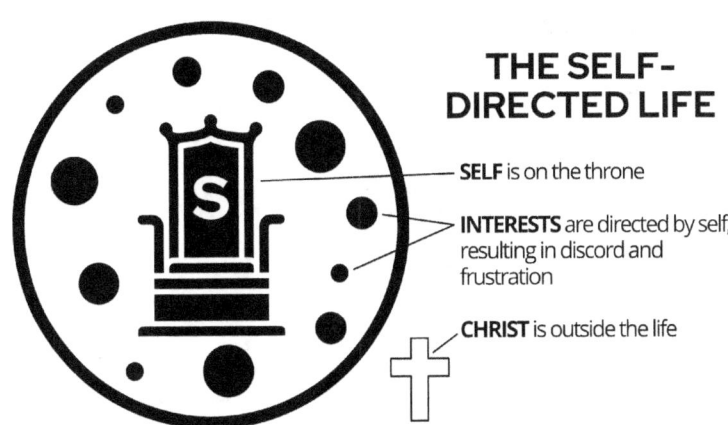

**THE SELF-DIRECTED LIFE**

— **SELF** is on the throne

— **INTERESTS** are directed by self, resulting in discord and frustration

— **CHRIST** is outside the life

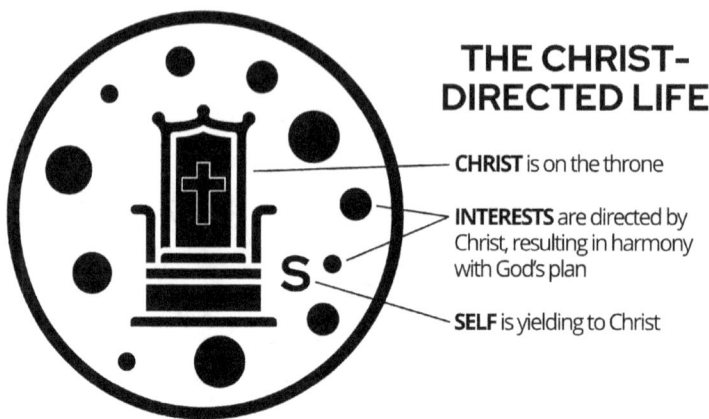

## THE CHRIST-DIRECTED LIFE

CHRIST is on the throne

INTERESTS are directed by Christ, resulting in harmony with God's plan

SELF is yielding to Christ

Which circle best represents your life? Which circle would you like to have represent your life?

## The following explains how you can receive Christ:

### You Can Receive Christ Right Now by Faith Through Prayer

(Prayer is talking with God.)

God knows your heart and is not so concerned with your words as He is with the attitude of your heart. The following is a suggested prayer:

> "Lord Jesus, I want to know You personally. Thank You for dying on the cross for my sins. I open the door of my life and receive You as my Savior and Lord. Thank You for forgiving me of my sins and giving me eternal life. Take control of the throne of

my life. Make me the kind of person You want me to be."

Did you pray this prayer?

If yes, please email relationshipsgodstyle@yahoo. com sharing your decision, along with your address, to receive a special FREE gift.

## How to Know That Christ Is in Your Life

Did you receive Christ into your life? According to His promise in Revelation 3:20, where is Christ right now in relation to you? Christ said that He would come into your life and be your friend so you can know Him personally. Would He mislead you? On what authority do you know that God has answered your prayer? (The trustworthiness of God Himself and His Word.)

### The Bible Promises Eternal Life to All Who Receive Christ

"And the testimony is this, that God has given us eternal life, and this life is in His Son. The one who has the Son has the life; the one who does not have the Son of God does not have the life. These things I have written to you who believe in the name of the Son of God, so that you may know that you have eternal life."

*1 John 5:11–13*

Thank God often that Christ is in your life and that He will never leave you (Hebrews 13:5). You can know based on His promise that Christ lives in you and that you have eternal life from the very moment you invite Him in. He will not deceive you.

## An important reminder...

### Do Not Depend on Feelings

The promise of God's Word, the Bible—not our feelings—is our authority. The Christian lives by faith (trust) in the trustworthiness of God Himself and His Word.

This train diagram illustrates the relationship among fact (God and His Word), faith (our trust in God and His

Word), and feeling (the result of our faith and obedience) (John 14:21).

The train will run with or without the caboose. However, it would be useless to attempt to pull the train by the caboose. In the same way, we as Christians do not depend on feelings or emotions, but we place our faith (trust) in the trustworthiness of God and the promises of His Word.

## Now That You Have Entered Into a Personal Relationship With Christ

The moment you received Christ by faith, as an act of your will, many things happened, including the following:

1. Christ came into your life (Revelation 3:20 and Colossians 1:27).

2. Your sins were forgiven (Colossians 1:14).

3. You became a child of God (John 1:12).

4. You received eternal life (John 5:24).

5. You began the great adventure for which God created you (John 10:10; 2 Corinthians 5:17 and 1 Thessalonians 5:18).

Can you think of anything more wonderful that could happen to you than entering into a personal relationship with Jesus Christ? Would you like to thank God in prayer right now for what He has done for you?

By thanking God, you demonstrate your faith.

To enjoy your new relationship with God...

## Suggestions for Christian Growth

Spiritual growth results from trusting Jesus Christ. "The righteous one shall live by faith" (Galatians 3:11). A life of faith will enable you to trust God increasingly with every detail of your life, and to practice the following:

**G** Go to God in prayer daily (John 15:7).

**R** Read God's Word daily (Acts 17:11)—begin with the Gospel of John.

**O** Obey God moment by moment (John 14:21).

**W** Witness for Christ by your life and words (Matthew 4:19; John 15:8).

**T** Trust God for every detail of your life (1 Peter 5:7).

**H** Holy Spirit—Allow Him to control and empower your daily life and witness (Galatians 5:16, 17; Acts 1:8).

## The Importance of Baptism

The view of most evangelical Christian scholars is that salvation is by grace through faith alone. This is especially indicated by Ephesians 2:8–9, John 3:16, 1 John 5:1. It is important to understand that baptism is a result of salvation, not a cause.

There are different baptism methods. They may include the sprinkling of water over the head of the professing believer or the total immersion of the person under water (Greek: "Baptismo" means to immerse). However, the procedure is not as important as the individual's understanding and motivation to seek baptism.

Some cite Mark 16:16 as their proof text that baptism is necessary for salvation, but they only quote the first half of the verse and typically leave out the second half, which indicates the necessity of belief as being the prerequisite to the salvation issue.

The way to resolve most problems pertaining to the issue of baptism is to look at the whole of Scripture. When we do, we find that there is absolutely nothing we can do as humans to earn salvation. Romans 6:23 tells us that salvation is a "free gift." Free means that there is nothing we can do to deserve it. On the other hand, baptism is something we choose to do. If baptism or any other human work or activity (such as going to church regularly, going on a pilgrimage, or visiting a "holy site") contributed to our salvation, we could boast that we did something and contributed to our salvation. However, Scripture says that no one should boast before God (Ephesians 2:8–9).

We come to Christ though grace by faith, and our public baptism brings glory and honor to God. Baptism is an act of obedience, not to obtain salvation, but because of it—because we love Him and want to obey Him. The motivation to pursue baptism should originate from a desire to show to the world an outward demonstration of the person's decision as well as the inward work the Holy Spirit has already begun in us. An unsaved person would not likely want to be baptized because he would not have the Holy Spirit indwelling him to prompt his desire to follow Christ in obedience (unless a sect or cult group has erroneously taught him or her otherwise). The fact that one even wants to be baptized (being assured that only faith alone in Jesus Christ saves) is evidence that the Holy Spirit already indwells that person, a result of being born of the Spirit by faith alone.

In the book of Acts, baptism is typically the outward response to coming to faith. It was seen as part of a process which includes: 1) hearing (or reading about) the gospel, 2) being convicted and led by the Holy Spirit to confess one's sins (Greek: "Homologeo" means to agree with, to speak the same), 3) coming to faith in Jesus Christ as Savior, 4) beginning the progress of growth (which includes repenting from known sin), 5) joining a group of believers or church fellowship, and 6) being baptized. The last two parts are where there are different opinions among believers or churches.

Where some churches differ with what has been stated above chiefly centers on whether a person is saved if they have not been baptized (or if they have not been baptized the "right" way). In our understanding, a person is saved when they put their faith in Christ. Of course, we all want them to join a church which exalts Christ and be baptized.

## Fellowship in a Good Church

God's Word admonishes us not to forsake "our own meeting together" (Hebrews 10:25). Several logs burn brightly together; but put one aside on the cold hearth and the fire goes out. So it is with your relationship with other Christians. If you do not belong to a church, do not wait to be invited. Take the initiative; call the pastor of a nearby church where Christ is honored and His Word is preached. Start this week, and make plans to attend regularly.

*The Four Spiritual Laws Written by Bill Bright.*
© *1965–2013 Bright Media Foundation®*

www.ingramcontent.com/pod-product-compliance
Lightning Source LLC
Chambersburg PA
CBHW070647130626

46555CB00006B/2749